SILK FLOWER GOODBYE

Sage Gordon-Davis

Copyright © 2019 Sage Gordon-Davis
All rights reserved.

First print edition, 2019

ISBN 978-0-620-85626-3

www.sgdwrites.com

Dedicated to

Oupa Dennis and Granny Edith
For what was

Noleen
For what is

Cheri-lee
For what might have been

Acknowledgements

To my husband, Sean - thank you for understanding and enabling my writing time, for loving and supporting me, and for making sure that we have never gone hungry. To Darwin and Faraday, for being the most adorable distractions around. Dogs are people too.

To my family, Barry, Natalie, Danie, Alexander, and Denise; my in-laws, Donna, Colin, Leigh, Charlie, and Lilly; Aunty Trish and Uncle Guy, and Aunty Debbie and Uncle Steve - thank you for being, just being. Family is everything.

To Vicky, Nicole, Lauren, Werner and Rhianan, and Gavin and Deborah. Our shared joys and sorrows were the seeds of this project. Your friendship, love, and support have been the soil, sun, and water that grew it. Without you this book would not have happened. Thank you.

To Greg and Mike, Craig and Kim, CJ, and Ducky, the friends who have seen me at my most distracted, distraught, and disastrous - and stuck around anyway. Thank you for not giving up on me.

To Irene, thank you for encouraging me, laughing and crying with me, making sure I didn't lose my mind, always speaking the truth no matter how hard it was, and giving me some very necessary kicks up the behind.

To the writing groups who have kept me (relatively) sane and talked me out of giving up on more than one occasion, thank you all. If I had to name each member individually, this section would be longer than the book itself, so please forgive me for lumping you all in together. To the Wishful Inkers, thank you for keeping me on track with proper deadlines and challenging prompts, and for writing good words for good causes. To the Clarens writers, for allowing me to get off-topic at every meeting, and for coming back anyway, thank you. To the Bestexperimates, thank you for being the actual nicest people on the interwebs. And to the Wanderimos, what else can I say but "sjoe"? It's been a journey. Thank you, thank you, thank you.

To my teachers and mentors - Mark Stay, Mark Desvaux, and Tim Clare. I've written and rewritten this paragraph so many times and nothing is quite good enough to express everything that you've done for me (and for all the other writers you inspire and encourage). In the absence of a better way to thank you, I'll just say this - you're proper gents.

To Robyn - you belong in so many categories on this list, the only way to do this properly was to give you your own paragraph. Thank you for being my critique partner, my beta reader, my editor. Without you, this book would be a pile of poems in a desk drawer. Thank you for being serious about things that call for seriousness. Thank you for being silly about silly things. Most importantly, thank you for being my friend.

And to the wee babs Ellie, Sebastian, Hailey, Lilly, Ayla, Celine, and all those not yet born or thought of. Thank you for giving us hope. The future is yours, and there is no limit to what you can do with it. Don't let the rest of us muck it up for you.

cloud party

mist
hangs low
clouds that have
come to
dance with the earth
stayed out too late
with grassy fields
and
faced with the
hard and disapproving gaze
of early morning sun
forgotten
how to get home

life through the screen

sometimes
i see the notifications
the light flashing on my phone
and i think
do i really
do i really need this?
do i really want this?
do i really
have to be connected
24/7
all of the time
reachable
accessible
contactable
100% there
instead of 100% here?
do i really
need to post another picture
of my dog
my desk
my dinner
and do i really
want to see another
picture of yours?
do i really
want to live my life through the screen?
and then i
pick up the phone
and do it
anyway

human

skin and
blood and
flesh and
bone
the recipe
for a body
add soul
to make it
human

the way we talk

the way we talk
shapes the world we see
the language we use
makes it real
and when i hear
people around me
speaking
something i don't understand
i'm jealous
how different is the world
through the eyes of someone else
whose culture and beliefs
and traditions
and tongue
are different from mine
and i want to learn
to experience
to see
what they see

untouchable

when i move forward
it does too
flitting away from me
always
just out of reach
and it would be so easy
to give up
stop
walk away
but somehow i can't do it
i just keep looking
and reaching
and moving
in the belief that
one day
it'll get tired of me chasing
and it'll give up
and i'll catch it

red

red is not my favourite colour
though it was once
long ago
when i was
young
impetuous
rash
untempered
a fire-breathing
scarlet-passioned
whirlwind in human form

in this moment

in this moment
all i want
is a warm fuzzy blanket
a cup of hot chocolate
my dogs at my side
and a book to read
maybe some socks
thick comfortable ones
and fingerless gloves
so i can still turn the pages
but keep my hands warm

if we

if we
listened a little more
spoke a little less
spent some time
just learning
just being
with each other
instead of
always
trying to be
the smartest
the brightest
the loudest
if we tried to be
happy
instead of
right
wouldn't our worlds be
a little bit better

sweater

warm
soft
cozy
snug
like being wrapped in
lovely things
like
unicorn smiles
and kitten dreams
and fluffy angel wings
sweaters are
a personal
portable
wearable
hug

judge

i try not judge
not because
i'm afraid of being judged
but because
i know what it's like to be judged
i know the silent stares
that burn like ice
i know the argumentative
"but what if" and "but you really should"
no
i don't want to be that kind of person
who gets their high from others' lows
who punches down instead of lifting up
i try not to judge
it isn't always easy
i don't always get it right
but i try
your life is yours
not mine
do you
be who you are
and while you're at it
let everyone else do the same

people being people

i don't believe in
women's work
the way some people do
thinking that
somehow
a man's hands
can't get wet doing dishes
or pick up a child
or make a meal
i don't believe in
a man's duty
the way some people do
thinking that
somehow
a woman's hands
can't get dirty changing oil
or earn a cheque
or pay a bill
that somehow
what's between our legs
makes our hands different
makes our minds
different
i don't believe
that we aren't capable
of doing exactly whatever the hell we want
of being exactly whatever the hell we want
men and women
and anyone who sees themselves somewhere in between
just people being people

radio

turn the dial
and crackle through
someone reading the news
a farmer has grown a turnip
that looks like a man
turn the dial
and crackle through
a choir singing
songs for praise
that make you want to sing along
turn the dial
and crackle through
a weather report
cold front moving in
keep the fires going
turn the dial
and crackle through
a radio play
darling, don't leave
but i must, my love
turn the dial
and crackle through
people's lives
told in tiny bites of sound

on the bus

i stare out the window
it's what you do on a bus
to avoid making
unwanted eye contact
with randoms who might
try to hurt you
or think you want to hurt them
i don't want that
so i stare out the window
and the bus passes through
suburbs
streets of houses
with manicured lawns
and perfect porches
i stare out the window
and imagine the lives
of the people who live there
i see magic for them
in my head
because there isn't any
in my life
and i know
it has to be
somewhere

how dare you

how dare you
tell me
who i am
who i may be
who i ought to be
my identity is mine
i have fought for it
i will fight for it
i am good
even if i don't look pretty
i am kind
even when i'm not smiling at you
i am strong
even when i'm hurt
so how dare you
tell me who i am

society says

society says
i'm a woman
they say that's who i am
the lumps and bumps of my body
tell them that i'm not a man
but society can't see the inside
no, they can't see my soul
where i know that i'm neither
i'm just me
trying to be whole

destruction

destruction
everywhere i look
the debris
of things that were
and things that should have been
detritus
of a life spent
waiting for things to happen
for someone to throw down a rope
instead of breaking down the wall
shards of
possibility
what may have come to pass
if only
i weren't paralyzed
by the fear of
actually
making it

proud

i said that i would
do this
i made the claim
out loud
and now there's people
watching
in my mind there is
a crowd
they're staring as
i write this
and they're yelling
make us proud!

slow down

slow down
it's okay to not be first
and not be best
enjoy the time
enjoy the challenge
the medals and prizes
don't matter
slow down
and see what's around you
take it all in
there's no time like now
and it might not be there
when you're done
slow down
breathe
live
this is where you belong
where you are right now
and you are enough
just exactly as you are

street signs

it's odd to me
how we choose to immortalise
who we choose to immortalise
by giving their name to streets
and in fifty years
or twenty years
or fifteen years
or five
when they are no longer in favour
or their politics are found
unpalatable
we choose to immortalise
with money that could feed the hungry
clothe the naked
educate
rehabilitate
facilitate
someone else who fits the mood
for the next fifty
twenty
fifteen
five
and then it starts at the beginning again

different

you're different
and i don't understand

you're different
and it frightens me

you're different
and i can't stand it

you're different
and it angers me

you're different
so you're bad

they never look at the same
we strive for the same

food, water
love, home
safety

and the chance to be

hibernate

human beings should hibernate
when winter days mean
getting up in the dark
with fingers frozen
teeth chattering
knees knocking
leaving in the dark
in ice and slush
and wind that bites and howls
a ravenous beast
coming home in the dark
as cold as ever you were
expelling clouds from your lungs
and going to sleep in the dark
well that
at least
is normal
and at least the bed is warm
human beings
should
hibernate

stretch

stretch
breathe into it
relax into it
grow into it
become
whole
entire
of yourself
and know
who you are
in the moment
that is
be
as you are
here and now
without pretence
without pressure
stretch
into yourself

shuffle

we shuffle forward
the shambling horde
the waking undead

we shuffle forward
inch by inch
step by step

we shuffle forward
crawling upright

we shuffle forward
for minutes
that feel like hours
and hours
that feel like days

all this
queuing
waiting
wasting time and energy

for the cashier to say

sorry ma'am
you can't pay by card

our systems are
offline

bare

a single thread
unravels
in the story that you've
woven
it pulls and pulls
and suddenly
the truth
the thing you were covering
is stripped
and laid out
bare

liquid amber afternoon
(for Shelby Britton)

liquid amber afternoon
the last languid gasp of summer
before the leaves turn
gold
and red
and umber

one last dripping ice cream cone
cold and delicious
running white on sticky hands

one more leap
through splashing sprinklers
shrieking with laughter
in the refreshing spray

home again when the lights come on
and tomorrow is
something new

in my head

i spend too much time
in my own head
trying
to unravel my thoughts
the gordian knot
that keeps me stuck
where i am
trying
to decode my feelings
the unbreakable cipher
that keeps me guessing
i'm sorry i'm weird
and a little
unapproachable
i spend too much time
in my own head

grown pain

there's so much i want to say
but never will
because it'll hurt you if i do
it hurts me that i don't
but
sometimes
it's better not to say
everything i think
everything i feel
to talk
indiscriminately
about what i want
and what i need
when there are bigger issues at hand
sometimes
it's better for me to
swallow the little pains now
than watch you suffer them when they're grown

inspiration

inspiration is like snow
when i was young it
fell everywhere
on every surface
at a moment's notice
now it hardly falls
at all
though winter is still here
and i watch
and wait
and hope for it
but what comes is
not so much snow as
frozen rain
in short
sharp
showers
that melt before they touch the ground
no more fluffy snowfalls
in the global warming of middle age

forward

there's so much
wrong
in the world
so much
hurt
so much
hate
and now they're saying
that the people
fighting back
are terrorists
for
standing up
pushing
against the tyranny
against the hate
against the hurt
when that is the only way forward

social overwhelm

it's not that i don't like you
i'm sure i really would
but to go out there
and meet with you
is just something i never could
bring myself to do
it's loud out there
so noisy
there's so many people
too
and i'm comfortable
just where i am
where i can be
quiet
alone
and really just me

space

if only i could find
a little piece of quiet
some solitude
for my soul
to rest
to breathe
to refill
and take stock
without the bustle
without the noise
without the constant
annoyances
it's not that i need space from you
it's just that i need space for me

kindness

let kindness
be your default
do good
without thinking
help
wherever you can
whenever you can
however you can
it costs nothing
to be
generous with your spirit

dive in

dive in
plunge
into freezing waters
hold your breath
lungs aching
like you're being squeezed
all at once
by the world's biggest boa
feel small
feel insignificant
feel nothing
and
GO
swim
hard and fast
stroke and stroke and stroke
until you reach the water's edge
run to the fire
and warm yourself
having learned
what you can do
feel something
feel brave
feel powerful
dive in
plunge

reflecting

reflecting
rippling
resonating
patterns of light
on the surface of
something
darker
deeper
showing us
something
we can't otherwise see
giving us
the shape of it
but not the truth of it
because
reflections of the thing
are not
the thing itself
and that which wears the shape
of my face
is not
me

10,000ft

gold and tan and taupe
and emerald
becoming
rust and chestnut
nutmeg
cinnamon and sienna
and turning
mauve
and lavender
and heather grey
shifting cornflower and periwinkle
in the opaline distance
of the horizon
what adventures lie hidden

sensory overload

every sound is
magnified
multiplied
myriad
legion
overwhelming
storming the castle
and the poor lone sentry
can do nothing
but watch in
abject horror
unable
to protect
defend
attack
fight back
overloaded

aesthetic

squares upon squares
of aesthetic
dreams of
who we should be
made up stories
of lives we don't live
but for the cameras
everything is perfect
nothing is forgotten
but nothing is real
and that's fine
as long as
the filter
is right

belief

i never believed i would be here
with a house
and a husband
and a family
commuting in to work at a desk
i never believed

i never believed i would be here
past the age of 17
and when 17 came
and went
i thought
no, of course
it's 27 isn't it
i'll never make it past 27

i never believed i would be here
i made no plans
i spoke pie in the sky unreachable things
because it didn't matter
i would never make it to do them anyway
so why aim for
something achievable

and now i'm here
27 has been and gone
it's 37 now
and even with everything i've done
and everything i want to do
i still don't believe
i'll be here

finish line

the finish line
is so close now
i can see the
ribbon
in front of me
so close
it distorts the world
i can taste it
but no matter
how hard i work
i can't quite
seem
to get there

echo chamber

i talk to myself
inside my head
my voice goes on
sounds and
rebounds
an argument
sung in the rouund
in the echo chamber
of my mind

first blush of sunrise

first blush of sunrise
streaks across the sky
while sleepy stars still hang
speckled
freckled
pale and bashful in the light
promise of a warm and wondrous day

sprint

racing against myself
trying to be better
than i was
yesterday
hoping that i
can grow
and do good
and improve again
tomorrow
and doing the best
that i can
for today
because nothing
comes from nothing
and there's no gain
in staying the same

poison

we poison our minds
and our hearts
and our souls
every day
when we tell ourselves
the stories that
keep us down
when we tell ourselves
we're not good enough
not thin
or pretty
or strong
or smart
enough
we poison ourselves
with lies that
keep us blinkered
to our own possibilities

puppy

gentle snores
and
giant paws
and
floppy ears
and
snuggle near

it doesn't matter
how old you are
how big you get
you will always be
a puppy
in my heart

wouldn't it be nice

i don't need it
that perfect quiet space
so many of us
don't get that
the luxury of being
alone
with the thoughts
distractionless
and we work anyway
we get it done
in spite of
alarms
and pets
and chattering people
so
no
i don't need it
that perfect quiet space
but
oh
wouldn't it be nice

just fine

i
float in a cloud
a haze
a fog
that sticks and clings
and smothers
and as long as i
lie perfectly still
don't try to move
i can breathe
just fine

silk flower goodbye I

rose quartz and fizzy love hearts
and singing
loud
spinning arouund
black lace skirts
strawberry lips
love potion
horror movies and canvas sneakers
incense
electric guitars
so many colours
and all black
we were a contradiction
and there is no me without you

silk flower goodbye II

sunday morning hymns
more joy in them
than the way they're written
more laughter in us
than was right for the church
and the smell of magnolia
and baby powder
and chocolate cake
and coffee
the heat of the candles
dripping of wax
a different kind of magic
and there is no me
without you

silk flower goodbye III

walk in the garden
smell the salt air
and dream of open spaces where the soul can be free
nourish the mind
let it roam and grow
strength of spirit
willpower
smarts
heart
and there is no me
without you

silk flower goodbye IV

the scent of wool and lanolin
of horse chestnut and talc
of flour and butter and jam
some people might say
that you smelled of them
they're wrong
because wool
and lanolin
horse chestnut and talc
flour
butter
jam
these are the things that
smell of you
of the memories of home
and warmth and comfort

and there is no me
without you

sea food

fish and chips
salty
vinegary
in paper wrappings
gone translucent
from soaking
oil
through and through
good enough
on your
overstuffed couch
but
so much better
with our toes in the sand

last

does anyone else
remember
the significance of
the last rolo
well if you do
i want you to know
that this
is my
last rolo
and i'm sharing it
with you

stubborn

you are
stubborn
so
incredibly
infuriatingly
unimaginably
stubborn
but i can't blame you
that's the way you were made
that's the way you were raised
that's the way you were taught
if i'm going to blame
anyone
i guess it has to be
me
after all
you learned it
at home

open

don't you love me
he asks
but the asking isn't asking
it's telling

you will love me

yes i say
yes i love you

but you don't he says
if you did

he leaves the space open

o
        p
                e
                          n

open like he wants my legs

i love you
i say

then why
he asks

because this is mine
and i
am
mine
and it is you who does not love me

stay

i need you to stay
and i know it's selfish of me
but i can't lose you
i just
can't
after everything
i need you not to leave
i know
it's not something you want to do
it's not a choice you're making
but
please
if there's any way to
stay
don't go

both sides

sometimes we talk
and i feel
there is nothing about me
you don't know
nothing of you
hidden from me and then
you surprise me

smile a secret smile
and i feel
like i've never seen you before
we're starting again
everything new
perfect
untouched

and i love you with both sides of my heart

in a field

in a field
an archway blooms
a doorway to another world

he waits
in grey and lavender
for the woman
all in white
and smiles and cries at her beauty

words and rings and kisses
magic
binding souls together

and together they walk through

a doorway to another world
an archway blooms
in a field

understand

i need you to understand
what it does to me
when you
pretend that you're stronger than you are
that you aren't hurting or sick
that you don't need help
when i can see that's not true
and you refuse to care
for yourself
what you're telling me is
you don't care for me either
i'm not trying to guilt you
trip you up on your feelings
and trap you in mine
but if you can see that you're hurting me
and you say that you're not
then i don't see how we can
be

dragons

here be dragons
large green luminous
and threatening
and furious
and cold
the fights and frenzies
as yet unknown
the obstacles unseen
and also
tiny
sparkling and glimmering
speckled
shining
on the wing
the hopes and happinesses
still to come
in our relationship
here be dragons

phoenix

every time i sit down
to write for you
to you
about you
the words dry up inside my head
and i stumble over my own thoughts
i want to say
i miss you
i do
every day
and i'm sorry
that i wasn't the friend you deserved
so i'm trying
every day
to be a little more like you
a little kinder
a little sweeter
a little stronger
to believe that there's something
to make sense of it all

jumping off point

stand
at the edge of the jetty
watch the
freezing waters
below
churn and froth
and spray
wonder
who
has stood here
before you
and listened to the
waves
while the wind
whistles
whips your skin
with
salty tentacles
stand
and think
and wait
and
jump

quiet

there's a quiet
hiding
in the hustle of the house
in the sounds
of snoring sleepers
and the
deafening din of day
we carry on
we live our lives
we go
we do
we are
but there's a quiet
hiding
in our lives
in the space
where you used to be

wound

they say time heals all wounds
that's not true
i have a wound
made of guilt and regret
that festers in the murky waters of my grief
and seeps
and oozes
poisons my memories
so that all i remember
is not being there
not knowing
only saying goodbye
when it was too late

goodbye

i can't be angry
that i
didn't get to say goodbye
i was the one who stopped calling

i couldn't
because
it hurt too much
to hear your voices
when i couldn't hear hers

but i hope
you knew
that my not calling
was not the same as
my not caring

and i hope
you felt
my love for you
across
the silent distance

stuff

stuff
there's just
so much
stuff
everywhere
and how much
of it is
junk
things i'm keeping
for a maybe
a tomorrow that
never comes
or because it's
something
you gave me
and it
weighs
on my heart

unexpected

unexpected
the hope that came out of
a grey and miserable
saturday morning

unexpected
the friendship that followed
the laughter and tears
years upon years

unexpected
the joy of seeing
your happiest day
by your side

unexpected
the heartache caused
by circumstance and stubbornness

unexpected
the moment of our reunion
after all i'd said
and done

unexpected
the ease of our friendship
restored and stronger
than before

unexpected
the grief and the pain
of my life
suddenly without you

you

i don't know
if you ever knew
how very much you were
admired
respected
loved
adored
i didn't until i saw how
many people
came to say goodbye
and so many of them
said how
sad it was
how wrong it was
how deeply
heart-sickeningly
unfair it was
that you were gone
but
you aren't gone
because you're here
with me
always
in my heart
and in my thoughts
and in everything i do
you're here
and you always
will be

feelings

i have a lot of feelings
about the things that you have done
a lot of them aren't good
and a lot of them aren't fun
but it's not my place to tell you
how to live or what to do
how to grieve the loss we're grieving
you must do what's right for you
it's not my place to judge you
or to tell you that you're wrong
but inside i feel cut up that
you didn't wait too long
i have a lot of feelings
that it isn't right to share
because
no matter what i'm feeling
i wasn't even there

i tried

i tried
to fit some societal ideal
of what strength is
i tried
to do my grieving on the inside
to cry quietly
i tried
to keep my problems to myself
not to disturb
i tried
to be rational and reasonable
and keep it together
i tried
because that's what you would do
it's what you had done
i tried
and i failed

something stirs

something stirs
and slithers
serpentine
inside my soul
sickness
at your supine
smug sense of security
sardonic souunds
slip from spirit to lips
and a single
sour
scream
scrabbles to escape

last words

i don't remember your last words to me
when i got there you were
unable to speak
unable to think
unable to move
a shell of the woman who made me

who made me brave
because you were brave

who made me strong
because you were strong

who made me kind
because you were kind

who made me love
because you loved

and i don't remember your last words to me
but i know the last words that existed
unspoken
between us

i love you
it's okay

peach

i would like to
say that i'm okay
that
everything
is wonderful
and life's a peach
i would like to
but
life is not a peach
not everything is
wonderful
and i am not
okay
i'm not okay
but i am trying
and
one day
i will be

bereft

is it cold where you are?
i feel like it's cold
or maybe that's just my world
without you
you were heat and light
a spark in the night
a beacon
a lighthouse
a campfire
warm
the guide we didn't know we needed
until you were gone
and now we blunder in the darkness
helpless and drifting
boats on an endless midnight sea
nothing to anchor us
or show us the way
aimless
alone
and bereft

tuesday

it's not the big days that get me
that stop me where i stand
choking on memories
and streaming tears
it's not the birthdays
anniversaries
holidays
it's the random
ten past three
on a tuesday afternoon
when someone says something
does something
makes something
so unbelievable
that i feel i have to share it with you
and i remember
i can't
the punch in the gut of
not being able to call and ask
how much milk goes in this sauce
and the sudden realisation
of how long its been
since i last heard your voice

argument

i hear both sides of the argument
whether i want to or not
i have no say
it just
happens
i hear the
he said
she said
back and forth
and i wonder how
can people so smart
be so dumb
how is it that you can't see
that this argument
all the arguments
are
unimportant
that being right
is costing you everything

lilies

i try not to go there
not to be near
because when i do
the hole in my heart
gets a little bigger
remembering
how much it hurt you
that i didn't share in your joy there
that i didn't feel the power
the presence that you felt
how unhappy i made you
but
sometimes
it can't be avoided
and i do my best to think
instead
of the lilies at your funeral
left at the feet of our lady
by some prior attendant
falling
unaided by either hand or breeze
and imagine it was you
displaying your hatred of the flowers
even in death

beginning of the end

this is it
the beginning of the end
the slope
trending ever steeper
the point of no return
from here it's
round after round
and wave after wave
playing whac-a-mole with
little illnesses
little illnesses
that get bigger each time
and every recovery
takes a little longer
and 100% healthy gets further away
this is life now
doctors and hospital
and rows upon rows
of pills
and capsules
and injections
until the day when
there's nothing left to do
no more treatments to try
no more magic tricks
that day is coming
it could be years
but this
this is the beginning of the end

numb

i know it's selfish
but i had hoped that
when you went
there'd be a sense of relief
from the pain
because your suffering
hurt us too
and i felt guilty
for hoping that
for thinking of my pain
when yours was unbearable
for thinking of my comfort
when you had none
and then
you were gone
and i wasn't
relieved but
numb

pause

count out the silence
one
two
only the feeling of a
heartbeat
to show that time moves on
in silence
three
uncomfortable now
like the start of a toothache
that says something isn't right
four
five
six
the silence becomes
painful
gnawing
suffocating
as if even the air
has fled in
fear

pale yellow light

pale yellow light
weak and
sickly
filtering
into the day

a day of
i don't want to
do i have to
couldn't i just
maybe not

a day of
why am i here
wasting my time
don't even bother
whatever

a day
lacking substance
just
a passage of time
a marker to nothing
signaled by
weak and
sickly
pale yellow light

after

i don't believe in
after
i don't think i ever have
i think it's just
done
over
finished
no post-credits scene
no stinger
just a blank screen
that
feels right to me
but
i want to believe in
after
to see you again
even if it's only
a dream

hollow

there's a
gnawing
barbed wire
hollow
when i think of you
in the recesses of my heart
a jagged
you-shaped
emptiness
where you were
a part of me
now you've been
ripped away
and the edges of that
gaping wound
are raw and red
and just won't heal
and i
wish
that i was
numb

About the Author

    Sage Gordon-Davis is a writer, artist, and occasional wielder of witticisms. Sage loves food, board games, books, movies, and ink in various forms. They share a tumble-down cottage with their husband and two extremely beautiful, naughty but lovable rescue dogs. Cows, sheep, and chickens make occasional appearances.

    You can find Sage online as @inkandsage on Twitter, @ink.and.sage on Instagram, @inkandsagewriter on Facebook, or at www.sgdwrites.com where you can also sign up for their newsletter.

    If you've enjoyed this book, please consider leaving a review, telling your friends and family about it, or shouting about it on social media.

www.ingramcontent.com/pod-product-compliance
Lightning Source LLC
Chambersburg PA
CBHW021958290426
44108CB00012B/1119